SMITH

THE KING PENGUIN BOOKS

76

THE SCULPTURE OF THE PARTHENON

THE SCULPTURE
OF THE
PARTHENON

BY P. E. CORBETT

—

WITH FORTY PLATES

PENGUIN BOOKS

THE KING PENGUIN BOOKS

EDITOR: N. B. L. PEVSNER

—

PUBLISHED BY PENGUIN BOOKS LTD

HARMONDSWORTH, MIDDLESEX, ENGLAND

PENGUIN BOOKS INC, CLIPPER MILL ROAD

BALTIMORE, MARYLAND, U.S.A.

PENGUIN BOOKS PTY LTD, WHITEHORSE ROAD

MITCHAM, VICTORIA, AUSTRALIA

—

TEXT PAGES PRINTED BY

HAZELL WATSON AND VINEY LTD, AYLESBURY

PLATES MADE AND PRINTED BY

CLARKE AND SHERWELL LTD, NORTHAMPTON

—

—

MADE IN GREAT BRITAIN

FIRST PUBLISHED

1959

ACKNOWLEDGEMENTS

We are grateful to the following for
permission to reproduce drawings:

Professor Gorham P. Stevens (figure 1)
The Bibliothèque Nationale, Paris (figures 3–6)
The British Museum (figure 7)

They were redrawn for this book by
Mr Donald Bell-Scott, who also
drew figure 2

—

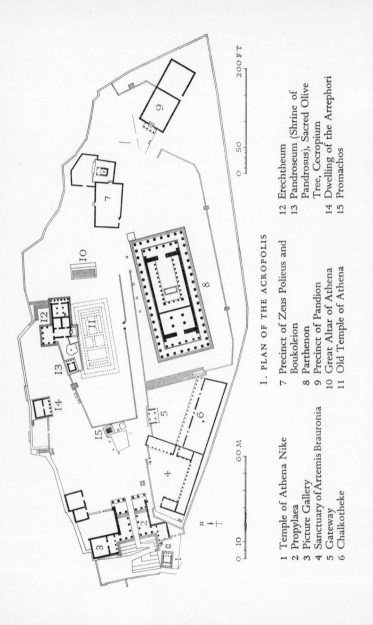

1. PLAN OF THE ACROPOLIS

1 Temple of Athena Nike
2 Propylaea
3 Picture Gallery
4 Sanctuary of Artemis Brauronia
5 Gateway
6 Chalkotheke

7 Precinct of Zeus Polieus and
  Boukoleion
8 Parthenon
9 Precinct of Pandion
10 Great Altar of Athena
11 Old Temple of Athena

12 Erechtheum
13 Pandroseum (Shrine of
  Pandrosus), Sacred Olive
  Tree, Cecropium
14 Dwelling of the Arrephori
15 Promachos

THE SCULPTURE
OF THE PARTHENON

IT is possible to enjoy and appreciate the sculpture of the Parthenon without regard to its original setting, but such an approach
is needlessly limited and forfeits the deeper insight and understanding which grow from the realization that it was designed for
a specific place on a particular building. We begin therefore with a
brief account of the Parthenon and its history; for the nature of
the building and the circumstances of its construction influenced
the choice of subject, the scale, treatment, and composition, while
a varied series of events, some happy, some disastrous, brought the
sculpture to its present condition.

The Parthenon was erected on the Acropolis or citadel of Athens
(Plate 1 and Figure 1) in the third quarter of the fifth century B.C.
and was dedicated to the goddess Athena, the city's divine guardian.
By that time Athens had not only recovered from the devastation
of the Persian invasion in 480 B.C. but had also achieved prosperity
and power as head of a league of Greek states, a league which
evolved by degrees from a voluntary alliance against Persia into an
Athenian empire. When active hostilities with Persia came to a
close, the statesman Pericles, who by then dominated the political
life of Athens, won popular approval for a great programme of
public works to give the city an outward appearance befitting, not
her present greatness, but the future; the project was to be financed
in part out of the surplus funds of the league.[1] In these plans
Athena was not forgotten; the sculptor Pheidias was commissioned
to create a colossal statue of her in gold and ivory, and the archi-
tects Ictinus and Callicrates began work on a magnificent new
temple in her honour.

Unlike a church or mosque, a Greek temple was not normally
designed for a congregation; it was primarily intended to shelter
the image of the divinity to whom it was dedicated, and to secure
his property, such as the sacred or precious vessels used in his cult,
or the votive offerings brought by his worshippers. It could serve
on occasion as a safe deposit; for individuals or communities might
entrust their valuables to the protection of a god. From another
point of view the building was in itself a votive offering, made in

7

gratitude for past benefits or in the hope of favours yet to come; it could at the same time be a manifestation of civic pride, to adorn the city in which it stood and to impress foreign visitors. A temple was normally oblong in plan, with the long axis lying East and West and the main door at the East end; the larger examples generally have a surrounding colonnade, but plan and orientation might vary to suit local needs and resources. The Parthenon lay East and West in the orthodox way, but its interior was unusual, since it was divided by a blank wall into two chambers of unequal size. The principal compartment, whose door was to the East, held the gold-and-ivory statue known from the Roman period onward as Athena Parthenos; the lesser chamber, opening to the West, was intended as a strong room to house the treasures belonging to Athena and, perhaps more important still, the accumulated revenue from the empire. In front of each doorway was a porch supported by six columns, and round the whole structure ran a continuous colonnade, with eight columns at front and back and seventeen on the long sides. The building, with its façade of eight columns instead of the more usual six, was exceptionally wide in proportion to its length, and it is probable that one reason for this was the desire to make the main chamber sufficiently broad to provide an ample setting for the Parthenos, the city's richest gift to its patroness. The same desire found expression in the quality and elaboration of the whole structure. It is built throughout of fine-grained local marble, and is in the Doric order, with fluted columns which taper upward; each one supports a spreading capital and square abacus, upon which rest the horizontal beams or architraves running from column to column. The architraves in their turn carry the metopes, panels of marble approximately four feet square; each is separated from its neighbour by a narrow grooved block or triglyph, and two metopes with their intervening triglyph fill the space between two adjacent columns, so that in all there were ninety-two metopes, thirty-two on a long side and fourteen on a short one. Above them runs a horizontal cornice; on the short side a second cornice rises with the gable end of the roof, framing a triangular space known as the pediment (Figure 2). The various elements which compose the Doric order are simple, almost austere; in the Parthenon, precision of workmanship, subtlety of form and the harmonious proportions of the whole combine with a complex system of refinements—delicate curvatures and inclinations of the main members—to create an air of vitality and resilient strength which has survived ruin and

8

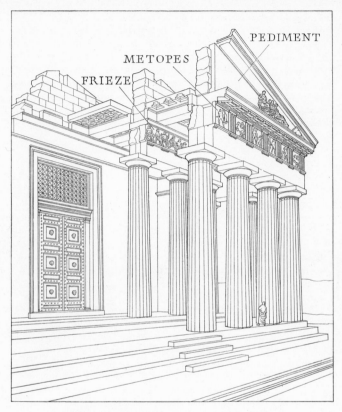

PEDIMENT

METOPES

FRIEZE

2. SECTIONAL DRAWING OF THE PARTHENON,
SHOWING THE POSITION OF THE SCULPTURE

restoration. This masterpiece of architecture was embellished with sculpture; all ninety-two metopes were carved in high relief, the two pediments were filled with groups in the round, and contained between them some fifty figures, and a frieze in low relief crowned the outer wall of the two main chambers of the temple, stretching the whole length of both long sides and continuing without interruption over the porches at East and West.

9

Ancient sources provide evidence for the dates when the various parts of the work were in hand. The annual accounts of the commission in charge of the building run from 447–6 to 433–2 B.C., and so presumably fix the beginning of work on the temple and its conclusion. The metopes were carved before they were put in place, and could only be installed before the roof was on; the gold and ivory statue was dedicated in 438–7, and the roof must have been weather- and burglar-proof during its construction, so we may conclude that the metopes were made between 447 and 439 B.C.[2] The blocks of the frieze, too, must have been laid before the roof was on; the sections on the long sides were carved in position, and can therefore belong to any time after the first few years of work; the balance of the evidence suggests that the West frieze was carved before its erection (though the conclusion is not unchallenged),[3] and on this view it too must date between 447 and 439 B.C. The pedimental figures were carved before installation; some were being made in 438–7, though we cannot prove that this was the first year of work on them, and as marble was still being quarried in 434–3, it is possible that some of them were not started until that year. Thus the metopes are the earliest, the pediments the latest, while the frieze comes between the two, overlapping both of them; the whole series was completed in fifteen years.

Between the fifth century B.C. and the present day the temple suffered serious damage on more than one occasion. About the middle of the fifth century A.D. it was remodelled, converted into a Christian church and dedicated to the Virgin Mary; on each long side portions of the frieze were removed to make room for windows,[4] the party wall between the two divisions of the interior was pierced, and the West door became the main entrance. The East door was blocked by the construction of an apse; in the process the great central slab of the East frieze was displaced and it was probably at this time that the East pediment lost its central figures. The Turkish conquest of 1456 had little effect, since only minor structural changes were needed to turn the Parthenon into a mosque. During the seventeenth century a number of travellers from the West visited the city and made drawings which record the appearance of the temple and of its sculpture at that time; these drawings are our main source of information for much that was destroyed in the catastrophe of 1687. In that year the Venetian general Morosini besieged the city; the Turks, relying on Frankish unwillingness to damage the Parthenon, stored their powder in it, but the ruse was betrayed by a deserter. The besieging force turned its artillery on the building, and at 7 p.m. on September 26th a great explosion blew out the long sides and the East end of the main chamber and wrecked the central parts of the North and South colonnades. The Turks were forced to capitulate, and Morosini, wishing to take part of the main group from the West pediment as a trophy, ordered his engineers to remove it; the first attempts brought some of the figures crashing to the ground, and the project was abandoned for fear of loss of life. In the following year the Venetian army had to withdraw from its conquests.

For over a century the ruined temple was neglected; a small mosque was built inside it and the accessible fragments were carried off as souvenirs, defaced by vandals and bigots, or burnt for lime. In 1799 Lord Elgin profited by his appointment as ambassador to Turkey to get permission for a party of artists and moulders in his suite to draw and take casts from the architectural and sculptural remains on the Acropolis. On realizing the speed with which those remains were disappearing or deteriorating he extended his plan by obtaining authorization to remove carved or inscribed marble fragments, and in the event succeeded in rescuing a substantial quantity of sculpture, much of which had fallen from the Parthenon;[5] Elgin's collection comprised the greater part of those figures and reliefs from the temple which have survived to the present day. The establishment in 1831 of the independent kingdom of Greece transformed the situation; much that had been lost was recovered through excavation, while conservation and restoration reduced to a minimum the chance of further damage.

THE METOPES

THE metopes were carved in high relief, some of the figures being virtually in the round; both the sculpture and its background were coloured, and some accessories such as weapons were added in bronze. The state of preservation varies very widely; all those at the East and West ends are still in place, though so heavily defaced by time, weather, and the hand of man that while it is possible to reconstruct the position of the figures, identify many of them, and form an idea of the general treatment, a judgement of their style and merit is scarcely within our power. The East end is devoted to a single story: the war between the gods and the giants, the mighty children of Earth, who tried to storm Mount Olympus. Although rigid symmetry is avoided, the fourteen metopes form a unified composition, whose centre comes above the main entrance to the temple. On the West, too, there is a single theme, a battle between Greeks and Amazons.[6] Greek legend told of more than one conflict with these women warriors from the East, and the representation on the Parthenon may or may not refer to the story that they invaded Attica and besieged the Acropolis until defeated by the Athenians under their king, the hero Theseus. A general movement from right to left runs through all fourteen metopes, on which mounted figures alternate with couples fighting on foot. For the central parts of the two long sides we are dependent on the drawings made before 1687, and much of the detail escapes us. The metopes at either end of the North side are still on the building, almost all of them severely battered; the theme was the Sack of Troy, but other subjects seem to have been interpolated in the middle.[7] On the South side, unity of theme was again avoided; no satisfactory interpretation has yet been given for the sketches of the central metopes, but it is at least certain that they had no direct connexion with those on either side of them, which depict the struggle between the Lapiths and the Centaurs. In all, eighteen metopes have survived from the East and West ends of the South side, fifteen of them in the British Museum, two in Athens, and one in Paris; their condition is good and their aesthetic qualities can be directly appreciated, so that they inevitably occupy the principal place in any discussion of the metopes.

The Centaurs, who were half man, half horse, were neighbours of the Lapiths, a people living in Northern Greece. They were invited to the marriage feast of Peirithoos, the king of the Lapiths, where they got drunk and tried to carry off the bride and the other women present. On the Parthenon the scene of wild disorder which ensued is split up into a succession of isolated pairs of figures, here a centaur victorious, seizing a woman or beating down an opponent, there evenly matched or overthrown. On metope xxvii, for example (Plate 2), a centaur turns to flight, pressing his right hand to the wound in his back; his opponent brings him up short, grasping his head with one hand. The artist has caught the Lapith in the fraction of a second before the blow descends; his left arm and leg are braced against the centaur's struggle to escape, but throughout the rest of the figure the muscles lift and swell in readiness, while chest and lungs expand with the effort, the tense body being thrown into even greater prominence by the swooping folds of the cloak. On the neighbouring metope (Plate 3) a centaur leaps in triumph over the corpse of his enemy; from his left arm hangs the skin of a wild beast—the cloak and its wearer are well matched—and behind his right shoulder are the fragmentary remains of a great wine-bowl which he has snatched up as a weapon. Amid the turmoil, a note of reflection, almost of pathos, is struck by the contrast between the exultant victor, obviously spoiling for another fight, and the crumpled figure at his feet. On both these metopes the execution does justice to the dramatic force of the composition; the modelling is vigorous and expressive, and the figures themselves fit so easily into the space they occupy that we are barely conscious of the limitations imposed by the square frame. The result is not always so happy; on metope XXXI (Plate 4) a centaur attempts to throw his adversary by grappling his calf and thigh with his forelegs, at the same time seizing him by the throat and making ready to strike with the other hand; the Lapith retaliates with a right cross to the head. The treatment of the anatomy is superficial and the blow unconvincing; the Greek seems like a lay figure, propped up by its right arm. There is rather more life in the centaur, and indeed the best feature of the metope is the creature's mask-like face, with its corrugated brow and matted hair. Yet the conception is a subtle one, with the animal and human parts of the centaur using different modes of attack, and the Greek punching like a trained boxer; one has the feeling that the man who carved these figures had been set a task beyond his knowledge or capacity. Nearer in merit to the two metopes discussed earlier on is the third one from the West (Plate 5). Once again a Greek seizes a centaur from behind, tugging at his head and forcing him down with one knee on his hind-quarters; here too the man is set off against the background of his cloak, though with less effect than on XXVII. The group has considerable vitality, but there is an element of stiffness in the poses, and the modelling of the anatomy is somewhat harsh.

These four examples illustrate the extent to which the surviving metopes vary in style and character; we have only a fraction of the original number, and it is quite likely that, if more were preserved, we would find an even greater range of stylistic development. Even as it is, at first sight the gap which separates the two extremes presents a problem; for instance, if the two human bodies on XXVII and XXXI (Plates 2 and 4) were detached from their panels and

13

came to us with no record of their origin, it might well be thought that one was fifteen or twenty years later than the other; yet the evidence for the construction of the building shows that the whole series of metopes was executed within the space of nine years at the outside. The apparent contradiction between this comparatively narrow period, fixed by objective evidence, and the wider interval suggested by considerations of style, is resolved when we observe that the metopes which are stylistically least developed also give an impression of feebleness and lack of vitality, deficiencies quite foreign to the major works of the first half of the fifth century; the explanation must surely be that they were the work of less talented, perhaps older, men, who had not mastered the innovations in the rendering of movement, drapery, and the human body achieved by their more progressive contemporaries. The Periclean building-programme was a vast undertaking for the limited man-power available, and even in antiquity the combination of speed and excellence with which it was accomplished excited astonishment and admiration; one can well imagine that the Parthenon alone severely taxed the city's resources of sculptors and masons. There must have been the temptation to enrol anyone who seemed reasonably qualified, and, until the work was well under way, the authorities could have little tangible evidence to modify their original assessment of the competence and reliability of those under their direction. Moreover, the fact that on the East and West sides the metopes do not stand alone but form parts of a carefully integrated whole, warrants the belief that they were produced in accordance with a master-plan which fixed the pose of the individual figures and the general lines of the composition (if nothing more), and it seems reasonable to conclude that the same is true for the long sides; yet although the general layout of a panel was pre-determined, the sculptor responsible for the translation of the design into stone seems to have enjoyed a considerable degree of freedom. Possibly the commission in charge took some time in settling down to its work and in making its control effective; it may also be that the necessity for a close scrutiny of details was not at first appreciated. All these factors may have contributed to that diversity, that wide variation between excellence and mediocrity, which is one of the most striking features of the metopes.

THE FRIEZE

THE frieze was about thirty-nine feet above floor level, and until the spectator came close to the building it was masked by the architraves of the outer colonnade, so that the angle of view was extremely steep (Figure 2). Moreover, the lighting was restricted; direct daylight from below was augmented by light reflected from the marble surfaces immediately above and in front – conditions under which sculpture does not show to best advantage. The limitations of the lighting are minimized by the brilliant sun and clear air of Greece; the upper parts of the figures on the frieze are carved in higher relief, in an attempt to compensate for the acute angle of vision, and the extensive use of colour doubtless made the figures stand out more boldly than they do today, but many fine details can be seen only on close inspection, and would have been obscure or invisible in their original setting.

The blocks which form the frieze are about three feet three inches in height; out of an original total length of about five hundred and twenty-four feet, over four hundred and twenty have survived, a further fifty-six feet are known from the drawings made by early travellers, and forty-five feet are lost. Despite the gaps and the damaged state of some stretches, the general condition is such that we can form a clear and trustworthy conception of the effect of the frieze as a whole, and at the same time assess the relative importance and quality of the various elements which compose it.

The whole frieze is devoted to a single subject, the Panathenaic procession. The Panathenaea, as its name suggests, was a festival in honour of Athena; as in many Greek festivals, contests of athletics, music, and dancing played an important part, but the event which gave meaning to the occasion was the solemn procession, formed from representatives of all classes of the community, which ascended the Acropolis to offer sacrifice to the goddess whose name the city bore. It was the outstanding event in the official religious calendar of Athens and took place annually in late summer, on the day said by tradition to be the birthday of the goddess, but every fourth year was marked by an important addition to the ceremonies: the primitive wooden statue of Athena which stood in another temple on the Acropolis was draped with a new robe, woven according to a time-honoured pattern. This robe, the peplos, was carried through the lower town and up to the citadel, escorted by a procession of greater size and splendour, and this quadrennial festival was distinguished by the title of the Great Panathenaea.

The frieze begins on the West side of the temple (Plates 21A to 25) with cavalrymen getting ready for parade; we see them fastening their boots or making last-minute adjustments to a cloak or wreath, preparing to mount or already mounted and moving off to form up. There is a considerable variety of costume; one man has only a simple cloak, fastened at the throat, another wears a short tunic, cloak, high boots, and a Thracian hat with long lappets; sometimes there is the armour which one would expect – a leather cuirass worn over a short tunic, and a plumed helmet – but elsewhere the combination of tunic, cloak, and broad-brimmed sun-hat gives, to modern eyes at least, an unmilitary look. There are, of course, no stirrups, for they were not invented until much later, but it is perhaps surprising that there is no sign of a saddle or saddle-blanket, although these were widely used in the classical period; they may have been painted on, but more probably the designer of the frieze chose to omit them. Reins and bridles were represented in some places by paint, in others by bronze attachments, and the holes for the latter often show quite plainly. The action unfolds from right to left; for a third of the side there is not a single mounted man; then riders predominate and the tempo increases until we come to the leading horseman, who looks round impatiently for the rest of his troop (Plates 20B and 31). In front of him stands a figure wearing a carefully draped cloak, the first of the stewards whose duty it was to control the procession (Plate 21A). Around the corner of the building, at the start of the North side, there is one last glimpse of the preparations (Plates 20A–21A) – a youth checks his horse with one hand and settles his wreath with the other as he stands waiting for a groom to finish fastening his companion's belt; but from here onward the ride-past is in full swing (Plates 16B–20A). The first impression is of a great mass of cavalry passing in compact and uniform array, but after a little one realizes that the pace varies from a trot to a canter, and is sometimes reined in to a halt; indeed at one point a definite though momentary check is given to the forward movement by the figure of a marshal, who stands facing the column as he signals to the rear ranks to close up on the leaders (Plate 16B). The riders show the same variety of costume as on the West side, and subtle differences in the bearing of the horses and the carriage and gestures of the men contribute still further to that vivacious rhythm which characterizes this section of the frieze. The technique of sculpture in low relief is here pushed to its limits; the riders are shown six or even seven abreast, superimposed one upon the other. In consequence the various planes of the relief are often extremely shallow, yet by well-calculated modelling, which in some places is achieved by scarcely perceptible variations of the surface, the figures are given solidity, while the crisp precision of the contours obviates the risk that the individual might be absorbed into an ill-defined mass.

In front of the cavalry comes the next division of the procession, the chariots (Plates 14B–17A); at the time when the Parthenon was built, these had long ceased to be used for war in mainland Greece, and were employed only for racing and on ceremonial occasions. Each one is drawn by four horses; the crew consists of a driver, dressed in the long tunic traditional to his office, and a man with a shield and full armour, who displays his skill and fitness by leaping from the chariot and then remounting in full career. The movement slows down – one chariot is stationary, with an attendant at the horses' heads (Plate 17A) – then breaks into a gallop once more. The groups are spaced out, giving a breathing space after the close-packed excitement of the cavalcade, and the stewards, who regulate the pace or start back from the path of a restive team, heighten the effect of surging activity (Plates 14B–15B and 16A).

From this point onward the pace slackens to a walk. We come first to a group of elders (Plate 14B), who take the opportunity of a halt to settle a wreath or exchange a word of comment; then the procession sets off again, but more sedately, with a group of lyre-players and flautists (which is not illustrated here), preceded by young men bearing jars of water for ritual purposes, others with trays of offerings, and finally sheep and heifers for sacrifice (Plates 14A–15A).

On the South side of the building the procession again moves from West to East; broadly speaking it is a repetition of what we have already seen, though the component parts are by no means identical. Here too the opening theme is the ride-past of the cavalry (Plates 6A–7A); much is missing or severely damaged, and in the better-preserved portions the work seems more hasty, some details being unfinished; the horses are less fiery, and the individual is lost in the crowd, so that there is a touch of monotony. When we pass to the chariots the quality rises; in the first group that is well preserved the horses are barely moving, an armed man walks on

17

the near side, while in the background a steward raises his arm to halt the team behind (Plates 6B and 26). The intricate pattern formed by the horses' legs stands out against the broad mass of their bodies, and a further contrast is supplied by the lively drapery of the two men, while the modelling, especially in the human anatomy, is of exquisite refinement. The quietness of this group is succeeded by a burst of furious energy as the procession breaks into a gallop; the horses toss their heads, ears laid back and nostrils flaring, the charioteer leans his full weight on the reins to control them, while his companion's cloak streams out in the wind of their passage. As on the North side, the chariots are preceded by musicians and youths bearing offerings; this part of the procession is too fragmentary to be illustrated here, but the final section with the sacrificial cattle is well preserved. This time the victims are all heifers; there is the same escort of youths walking with the sedateness that the occasion demands, their cloaks draped with studied propriety (Plates 7B and 8A–9A). A touch of light relief is given by one of the animals, which makes a sudden lunge forward, straining at the rope and forcing the youth in its path to abandon his dignity for the moment. Just in front another beast lifts her head uneasily (Plate 27), and it is an attractive suggestion that in his *Ode on a Grecian Urn* Keats had this slab in mind when he wrote of 'that heifer lowing to the skies'. After this interlude order is restored, and from here on the procession moves to its goal with unruffled decorum.

On the East side the two streams of the procession converge. At the extreme left a marshal looks back and signals to those behind him, linking the scene to the figures round the corner; in front of him are girls carrying wine jugs, bowls for pouring libations, and other objects; the leading pair is empty-handed (Plates 8B–9B). Next are six men quietly talking (Plate 10A); there may be a distinction between those with sticks, who presumably were not in the procession but have been waiting to receive it, and the others who have just arrived. The corresponding section on the right is incomplete (Plates 12B–13B and 30); on the part which has survived is another line of girls, most of them carrying libation bowls, but one pair with an incense burner; they are met by stewards, one of whom signals across to the head of the column on the left. The four men beside them with shaggy heads and intense gaze (Plate 13A) have been interpreted as magistrates or as legendary heroes, ancestors of the people of Athens.

Two groups of seated figures, larger in scale than the rest, look outward at the two divisions of the procession. They are the twelve major gods of Olympus, with two younger divinities standing beside them. On the left, in the place of honour nearest the centre, is Zeus, ruler of the gods and father of gods and men; he alone has a throne with a back and arm-rests. Beside him sits his consort Hera, holding her veil in the traditional attitude of a bride; in the background is a winged girl who may be Victory or Iris (Plate 10B). Next is Ares, the god of War, his unquiet temper expressed by the restlessness of his pose; then the Corn Goddess Demeter, holding the long torch which was her attribute. Her right hand touches her chin; the gesture, in antiquity an expression of sorrow, alludes to her mournful quest for her daughter Persephone, who was carried off by Hades to the Kingdom of the Dead. In front of her sits Dionysos, leaning carelessly on the shoulder of Hermes, the messenger of the gods, who is dressed ready for the road with boots, cloak and broad-brimmed hat; a hole is bored in his hand for a herald's rod of bronze (Plates 10A–11A). On the right, in a position of importance comparable to that of Zeus, is Athena, watching the ceremonies performed in her honour; she had a bronze spear, attached by rivets, but as it is a festal day she has laid aside her helmet and her aegis lies in her lap. Beside her and turning to speak to her sits Hephaestus; his body and shoulders are powerful but a slight distortion of his ankles and the stick beneath his arm hint at the tradition that he was a cripple (Plate 11B). The bearded figure next to them is probably Poseidon, with a youthful pair who are surely Apollo and his twin sister Artemis; the goddess at the extreme right is Aphrodite, and against her knee leans her son Eros, who shades her with a parasol (Plates 12A–13A and 28).

In the centre, framed by the two groups of divinities, are five figures, a man and a boy folding up a large rectangle of heavy cloth, a woman taking a stool from a girl who carries it on her head, and a second girl with another stool moving up behind (Plates 10B–11B). For the key position of the whole frieze the artist has selected the climax of the ritual; the peplos, the new robe for the statue of Athena, has reached its destination and has passed into the care of a magistrate and his acolyte. The rest of the scene is obscure; the woman must be the priestess of Athena, and perhaps the best interpretation is that she is setting out the stools as a symbolic invitation to the gods.

The style of the frieze is far more homogeneous than that of the metopes, though differences of execution and quality reflect the disparity between the abilities of the numerous sculptors employed on the work. The most noticeable gap lies between parts of the West side and the rest; for example, on the third slab on the West side (Plates 20B–21B) the technique of relief sculpture is not fully mastered, the upper and lower parts of the bearded man are poorly integrated, and the attitude of the boy next to him is curiously forced. The evidence cannot be pressed too far; for it is difficult to postulate any great interval of time between such a group as the man controlling a rearing horse (Plate 32) and some sections of the cavalcade on the North side (Plate 29). The differences between them may be due to the fact that the cavalcade is built up of multiple planes, while the group consists of a horse and man in isolation. Thus, although it seems probable that work on the frieze began at the West end of the building, the carving of the other sides cannot have been long delayed.

The decision to apply a continuous band of sculpture to the Parthenon raised certain technical problems. The frieze is exceptionally long; over five hundred feet had to be filled, and it was impossible to reduce the number of figures by increasing the scale because their height was limited by the height of the blocks on which they were to be carved. The scene represented must therefore be one with a multitude of characters whose presence was essential to the action; to pad with extras and supernumeraries could only result in weakness and vapidity. It would not have been surprising if the artist responsible had decided to simplify his task by representing a different subject on each of the four sides of the building; for Greek taste did not always insist that a continuous frieze should have a single theme. We will postpone consideration of the reasons which may have prompted the selection of the Panathenaic procession as the subject, and simply note that one practical advantage of the choice was the number and diversity of the participants. Given the particular subject, it is still possible to think of several different ways in which it might be treated; as we have seen, the method actually adopted was to divide the procession into two streams, running parallel to each other from West to East on the two long sides of the building and meeting at the East end. The only way on to the Acropolis passes through the Propylaea, or gateway, at the West (Figure 1); from here the principal route in antiquity ran toward the North-west corner of the

Parthenon and continued along its North side, giving access to the area East of the temple; alternatively, a visitor could pass southward through a little gateway and then approach the building on its West side. It was possible to go round the South-west corner, but the most convenient and natural route lies on the North. Thus most people would see the West end and part of the North side at the same time, but they would not normally see the South and West sides together, so that the South-west corner is the most unobtrusive position for the division between the two streams into which the relief is divided.[8]

The composition and treatment of the different parts of the frieze vary according to their position on the building. There is no way into the cella on either of the long sides, and this part of the temple would normally be seen by people walking parallel to it from one end to the other; on the North and South sides the figures on the frieze move steadily from West to East with only minor checks and pauses. The entrances to the two divisions of the interior are at the East and West ends, and here the natural tendency would be to approach the central point of the side. At the West (Plates 21A–25) there is indeed a general movement and an increasing degree of readiness from right to left, which leads on to the continuous procession round the North-west corner, but the central point is marked out by a group of exceptional liveliness and quality – the man controlling a restive horse (Plate 32) – and there are a number of standing figures which provide a static element; several of them face to the right and save the side from being unidirectional, while the last three slabs on the right include a horse which is heading in the opposite direction from all the rest (Plate 24B); this animal, with the two men nearest the corner, facilitates the transition to the South side. At the East the artist has set above the main entrance a group that is worthy of its position (Plate 10B–11B); in the magistrate with the peplos and the priestess with the stools we see the moment of greatest solemnity at which the procession reaches its natural end. The necessity of bringing together the two streams which run along the North and South of the building lends itself to the formation of a unified composition that guides the eye to the middle; the seated divinities enclose the central group, lifting it above the plane of normal human life; their presence also creates a wide interval between the two converging lines of maidens, thus avoiding the awkwardness of a head-on meeting. The composition has however a weakness, which may at first pass unnoticed in the general excellence of the execution; the gods turn their backs on the central group, and though Apollo, Hephaestus and Hera look round at their neighbours, and so toward the middle, the abruptness of the division cannot be ignored. There is also a minor illogicality (Plates 10A–11A and 12A–13A); the gods are apparently conceived as ranged in a line or semicircle and watching the procession from the far side, yet the feet of the outermost divinities overlap on the near side of the standing figures. Similarly, in the West frieze (Plates 21A–25) the stationary and moving figures are all shown in the same plane, though here the difficulty is less obtrusive, because in general the various groups do not overlap.

Despite the distinctive treatment on the long and short sides, the frieze is an organic whole. The visitor walking along the building moved with the procession from its starting point to its goal; there seems also to be a movement in time, for it is hard to believe that the cavalry began their ride-past before they were all formed up; it would be logical to suppose that successive phases of the procession unfold in series from West to East, but this is perhaps too mechanical an interpretation for a work of art. It is indeed difficult to decide how far the frieze can be regarded as true to life; though the general character and many of the details tally with ancient statements about the Panathenaic procession and so support the identification of the subject, the agreement is not complete. Certain elements are missing which we know from classical authors to have formed part of the actual processions; the most striking instance is the absence of the citizen infantry in full armour. We are further hampered by the fact that, as is usual in Greek art of the period, interest is concentrated on the actors in the scene, and the setting is not indicated; at the most there is a rock to give support or purchase to a foot; everything else has to be supplied out of the spectator's own knowledge. Other sources make it clear that the procession started just outside the city, in the Ceramicus or Potters' Quarter, and that the peplos was taken up to the Acropolis; so we can locate the beginning and the end of the frieze, but the intervening points are left undefined, for the artist was not concerned with topography. The division of the procession into two streams has been taken to reflect an arrangement in real life whereby it split up and passed on either side of the temple; it is at least beyond doubt that the reliefs on the South side cannot be a faithful reproduction of the hypothetical southern portion, for apart from the

22

unlikelihood that the cavalry and chariots went on to the confined area of the Acropolis at all, neither they nor the sacrificial animals could negotiate the flight of steps which leads to the West end of the temple. The explanation is probably to be found in the vision of the artist, who saw in this treatment of the subject the most satisfactory solution for one of his problems. Again, the number of the victims shown on the frieze is a token figure, which falls short of reality; it is therefore possible that although the cavalry occupies so large a section of the sculpture, in real life it did not form so considerable a proportion of the whole procession. There would be an obvious advantage in an exaggeration of this kind: one of the difficulties was the amount of space to be filled; by their nature the groups of horsemen require a broad field if they are not to appear cramped, and at the same time they give ample scope for variety and invention, so that the theme could be extended and developed without the risk of monotony. Moreover, we cannot be certain that the sequence of the frieze mirrors the order of the parade; from West to East we pass from the secular display of cavalry and chariots to the dedicated victims, while on the East, where the gods are present, there are no animals; it is hard to believe that this progression is fortuitous. All these considerations prompt the belief that, although the frieze is based on actuality, the whole subject and its various components have been shaped and remoulded into harmony by a powerful and sensitive mind.

THE PEDIMENTS

THE pediments are over ninety feet long and about three feet deep, measured from the back wall; their height rises to over eleven feet in the centre. The space was originally filled with figures carved completely in the round, the largest of them being nearly twice life size. Although no account of the metopes and frieze has survived from antiquity, they are sufficiently well preserved for the subjects to be intelligible, but the principal figures from the pediments are either missing or shattered, and if we had only the material remains to guide us it is extremely doubtful if the themes of the two monumental compositions could be identified. Fortunately Pausanias, who wrote a Description of Greece in the second century A.D., states explicitly that the pediment above the entrance— that is, at the East–represented the Birth of Athena, while at

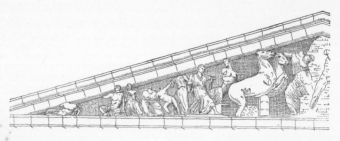

the other end was the contest between Athena and Poseidon for the land of Attica;[9] our knowledge is augmented by drawings made shortly before 1687.[10]

To take the West pediment first, the legend went that in the remote past Athena and Poseidon both claimed the prerogative of being the guardian deity of Athens and the surrounding countryside. The dispute was decided on the Acropolis, where the two gods wrought marvels to support their claims; Poseidon struck the rock with his trident, producing a spring of salt water, while Athena caused the first olive tree to spring up. Different versions of the story say that the decision was made by Zeus, by a jury formed from the gods, or by a legendary Athenian hero, but all agree that the verdict was in favour of Athena. Down to the Roman period the tokens brought forth by the contending gods were still shown on the North side of the Acropolis in and beside the Erechtheum: the marks of Poseidon's trident in the rock, a salt well, and an ancient olive tree.

The seventeenth-century drawing (Figures 3–4) gives a clear idea of the way in which the subject was treated. Attention is concentrated on the two main figures which fill the centre of the pediment, Poseidon starting back in amazement, Athena striding by with a gesture of triumph; the miraculous olive tree stood between them. Behind the contestants are their chariots, escorted by Hermes and Iris; the drivers are in the act of reining back the horses, for the two gods have leaped down, displayed their powers and decided the conflict even before the charioteers have had time to bring the teams to a standstill. In the corners other divinities or heroes sit and lie, intent upon the issue. The movement of the chariot groups offsets the strong centrifugal lines of the two main

24

PEDIMENT IN 1674

figures and at the same time emphasizes the breathless urgency of the scene; the excitement extends right to the corners of the pediment, where the two reclining figures raise themselves and swing round in their eagerness for a better view; a current of attention flows from the wings to the centre.

We are comparatively well informed about the general aspect of the composition, but the individual statues are extremely fragmentary. A draped torso (Plate 35) belonged to the figure which strode beside the right-hand chariot; she can be identified as Iris, for there are sockets in the shoulders for the attachment of wings. She wears a short tunic well suited to fast movement, made of a light, mobile material which is tossed in fluttering streams of folds or pressed close over thigh and stomach by the interplay between the air and the forward thrust of the body. The statue from the left corner of the pediment is particularly well preserved (Plate 33); the analogy of similar figures from the temple of Zeus at Olympia suggests that he personifies one of the rivers of Athens, perhaps the Kephissus or Ilissus. He has been lying at ease; stirred by the wondrous events which are taking place, he raises himself on his left arm and swings round to watch. The figure reveals a thorough understanding of the interplay of flesh and bone set up by this movement; the contrast between tensed and relaxed muscles, the distortion of the stomach and the asymmetry of the chest produced by the concentration of the weight of the body on the left arm are all carefully observed, but the artist has applied his knowledge of anatomy with restraint, sacrificing the elaboration of detail in the interest of overall unity and harmony. The principal figures are shattered, but enough remains of the upper part of Athena to illustrate their quality (Plate 34). The raised right arm is lost, and so

25

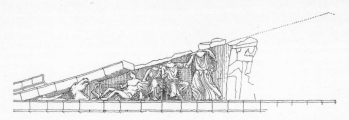

also is the face, though the back of the head and helmet is well preserved. Over her tunic the goddess has a narrow aegis, in which can be seen holes for the attachment of a bronze gorgoneion and a fringe of snakes; there is a deliberate contrast between the abstract pattern of the aegis, the full yet firm modelling of the right side and breast, and the heavy folds of cloth.

The story of the birth of Athena told how Hephaestus cleft the head of Zeus with an axe, whereupon the goddess sprang forth fully armed, while all Olympus wondered. It is a dark, obscure legend whose significance has been much discussed, though without agreement. A marked feature of the intellectual activity of the fifth century was the attempt to reconcile its heritage of primitive beliefs with a deeper and more developed conception of religion and morality; allegorical interpretation was among the methods employed, and as wisdom was one of Athena's main attributes, it may be that the more advanced minds of Periclean Athens understood the myth to mean that wisdom emanates from the highest divinity. The companion drawing of the East pediment (Figures 5–6) shows clearly that the principal figures had disappeared before the explosion, but a relief carved on a Roman altar now in Madrid is probably a modified reproduction of part of the missing group (Figure 7) so that we can form an idea of the way in which this difficult subject was treated.[11] The artist chose to represent the moment immediately after the event; Zeus sits enthroned in the centre, holding sceptre and thunderbolt, Victory flies down to crown Athena, who strides before him, while behind him is Hephaestus with his axe. To the left of Hephaestus are the three Fates, who from the moment of birth onward spun out the destiny of all, whether human or divine; the corresponding portion of the right half of the pediment is completely lost. The sculptures from

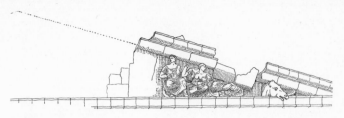

the two wings of the composition are comparatively well preserved, and the drawing shows their original disposition. On the left is a young girl, perhaps Hebe, the cup-bearer of Zeus; she starts back in alarm or surprise, and the sudden movement sweeps her long tunic into folds like the breakers of a heavy sea. Beside her are two seated goddesses; the nearer one, who is probably Demeter, twists round and raises her hands in wonder, while her daughter Persephone is motionless on the verge of realization and reaction (Plate 38). Their companion is a male figure half sitting, half lying on a rock with the hide of a panther or lion as a cushion (Plate 37); his identity is doubtful, but the skin and his proximity to the divinities of the grain and the earth which bears it warrant the suggestion that he is Dionysos. In the extreme corner the sun-god and his team break through the rippling surface of the sea; the horses snort and toss their heads as they begin their course (Plate 36). At the other side of the pediment, in the corresponding position to Demeter, Persephone, and Dionysos, are three nymphs or goddesses, two of them seated and the third reclining in the lap of her

7. ROMAN RELIEF WHICH SHOWS WHAT ARE PROBABLY
SOME OF THE MISSING CENTRAL FIGURES OF THE
EAST PEDIMENT

neighbour (Plate 39); once again it is impossible to say who they are, for the old belief that they are the three Fates had to be abandoned when it was realised that the Fates were probably represented elsewhere in the composition. In the angle of the pediment was the goddess of the moon in her chariot, sinking from sight below the horizon; only the heads of the horses were shown, and from the best preserved of these (Plate 40) we can see how the sculptor has re-thought the natural forms into a sequence of broad, well-defined masses and at the same time by subtle indications of fatigue suggested the labours of the journey which has just ended.

From the sixth century B.C. onward there had been numerous attempts to solve the problems of pedimental composition. As an inevitable consequence of the traditional forms of temple architecture, the space to be filled was a low isosceles triangle; the taste of an earlier generation accepted marked variations in the scale of the figures, and did not necessarily insist on an intimate connexion between the various parts of the pedimental group, but in the latter part of the sixth century, and still more in the fifth, a growing desire for unity and integration led to the acceptance of the principle that the whole field must be occupied by a single subject. In consequence major changes of scale were felt to be inappropriate and attention was concentrated on the alternative solution of adapting the pose to the position in the pediment, so that the principal characters stand, those next to them are crouched or seated, while the figures in the angles recline. This development went hand in hand with a greater feeling for composition, which stressed the importance of the main actors in a scene by placing them at the centre and grouping the subordinates around them. By the middle of the fifth century the requirements of a pedimental group were familiar and well understood, and the elements for a successful solution were to hand, but in the pediments of the Parthenon we find a new and outstanding quality; the artist's grasp of the problem is so sure that the attitude of the figures, their placing and interrelation, seem an organic growth arising from the situation and their part in it, not dictated by the architectural frame. In the West, minor divinities and legendary figures have settled themselves in readiness to watch the contest; the two competitors arrive, and in the centre all is bustle and turmoil, movement and counter-movement in a plane parallel to the rear wall of the pediment. In quick succession Poseidon and Athena show their powers; the onlookers are already alert and intent, and their reaction is immediate; the whole group vibrates like a taut wire with an involuntary stir of excitement. The East pediment has a deeper, more solemn tone. The Sun and Moon in the corners indicate both place and time; at break of day, with the whole firmament as a backcloth, the assembled gods sit or lie on Mount Olympus, withdrawn into unfathomable contemplation, when suddenly a new goddess bursts forth among them in all her power. The impact of her coming has not yet reached the wings, and the movement dies away in the outer groups (Plates 37, 38 and 39); the innermost seated figures twist round toward the centre, their immediate neighbours face outward on a line roughly parallel to the axis of the temple, while the reclining figures are set at a slight angle to the rear wall of the pediment. This change of orientation underlines the fact that the two outermost figures are as yet unmoved, and at the same time provides an easy transition from the centre to the angles. Despite the restricted space available, the groups are successfully composed in depth, in contrast to the more two-dimensional treatment to be observed in the West pediment. There is balance without rigid symmetry; two women and one man on one side, three women on the other; in one group the two seated figures are intimately linked, in the other the tie is closest between the reclining woman and the companion who supports her. There are differences of characterization, too; for instance, the flagging energy of the horse of the Moon complements the fire and freshness of the Sun's team as they take the bit between their teeth (Plates 36 and 40).

It is plain that for both compositions there must have been a master-plan which was worked out in considerable detail; the two groups have much in common – grandeur and boldness of conception, richness of invention, a thorough understanding of the technical requirements – but there are elements which perhaps reflect a difference of temperament and personality; however, where so much is missing or known only at second-hand, one cannot be certain that the two designs could not be by the same man. As regards the actual carving, the quantity of work involved and the brevity of the period within which it was completed leave no room for doubt that the execution of the figures was entrusted to a number of sculptors, and in the surviving portions we can distinguish the work of several different personalities; for example, Persephone and Demeter seem cold and over-intellectual beside the mellow opulence of the reclining woman (Plates 38 and 39). Yet considered as a whole the remains of the pediments show a remarkable uniformity of style and execution, as though they were produced by a team of outstanding artists who had worked long enough together to have absorbed a common tradition and made it their own; how far that style was the creation of a single, dominating genius, and how far it was augmented and expanded by individual contributions, cannot now be determined. The result is rightly regarded as a combination of artistic excellence and skilful, far-reaching organization, and it is all the more surprising to observe that the co-ordination appears to have broken down at an elementary, though vital, point; cavities and recesses have been hacked in some of the figures, an operation that was unquestionably carried out after the carving had been completed. There can be no doubt that these cuttings were made to enable the statues to be set more closely together, and the conclusion seems inescapable that there had been a serious miscalculation; the figures destined for the West pediment occupied too much space, and drastic adjustments were necessary to make them fit, which certainly altered the intervals between them and may also have modified their orientation;[12] the same difficulty may have occurred at the East end. For this reason, although there is good evidence for the arrangement of many of the figures in the pediments, some of the refinements of composition which have been detected can only be accepted with reservations, since that arrangement may not entirely correspond to the original design.

PHEIDIAS AND THE PARTHENON

The authorship of the sculpture is a complex question, of which only a brief survey can here be given. In the fifteenth century Cyriac of Ancona referred to the Parthenon as 'the marvellous work of Pheidias', and his opinion has since found many adherents; others have sought to reduce the part played by Pheidias to a minimum. On any view he can have done little or none of the actual carving, so great is the quantity of sculpture, so short the period in which it was completed. Plutarch, who lived in the first to second centuries of our era, is the only ancient authority for a connexion between the sculptor and the temple; in his *Life of Pericles* he enumerates many of the buildings which composed the Periclean programme and underlines the far-reaching organization of labour and supply which made them possible; he states that the record names Pheidias as the maker of the golden statue of the goddess, but adds, 'everything was virtually under his control, and he took charge of all those employed because of his friendship for Pericles'.[13] Co-ordination on such a scale takes a good deal of time and energy, and the Parthenos, forty feet high and richly decorated, was a major undertaking in itself; even so, a scholar of great knowledge and discrimination has argued that Pheidias had a guiding hand in the sculptures: 'He must have sketched the designs, or at least initiated and revised them'.[14] There are in fact three obvious directions in which his influence might have operated: on the style, on the general conception and composition, and on the choice of subjects.

As we have seen, the style of the frieze is comparatively homogeneous; the less developed metopes show a considerable diversity, while those which are more advanced come nearer to the frieze; in the pediments there is once again a greater range, but here the effect is of individual voices speaking a common tongue, rather than a variety of dialects. Taken together, metopes, frieze, and pediments illustrate the formation and development of a distinctive style which bears the hall-mark of a great artist, not a committee. Considerable progress has been made in the attempt to demonstrate a close connexion between this style and the work of Pheidias, but our knowledge of his work, though substantial, is second-hand and incomplete, resting entirely on Hellenistic and Roman copies of varying merit and reliability;[15] conclusions based on this evidence are at the most possibilities, not certainties.

Despite differences of treatment, the two pedimental compositions have sufficient in common to suggest that they were inspired by two minds of equal calibre, if not by the same man: grandeur of conception; individual figures welded into a unified whole without the sacrifice of their personality; fertile invention; a triumphant solution of the problem created by the rigid architectural frame. Although it is difficult to make a direct comparison between an uninterrupted zone in low relief and a self-contained group of figures in the round, the resourcefulness with which the composition of the frieze is adapted to the temple and its setting, the combination of rhythm and diversity in the component groups and figures, and the sense of organization which pervades the whole, are compatible with a common origin for frieze and pediments. At East and West the condition of the metopes is such

31

that we can say little save that in each case the fourteen panels appear to be units of a single plan; on the two long sides it is hard to detect any over-all pattern, but so much is lost that it is unsafe to dogmatize.

In subject the pediments have a close relevance to the temple which they adorned—in this respect, too, the Parthenon marks a great advance on earlier buildings; at the East, the advent of Athena, at the West, her establishment as guardian of the city. Moreover, the scene of one event, the conflict between Athena and Poseidon, is the very hill on which the temple stands; the anniversary of the other was the day of the procession to the Acropolis which is portrayed on the frieze. Greek legend ascribed to Athena a leading role in the victory of the gods over the giants, the theme of the metopes at the East end; more significant still, tradition required that a representation of this conflict be woven on the peplos, the new robe for the goddess, which has the place of honour above the East door. This many-sided relationship must surely be deliberate; we might therefore expect the metopes on the other three sides to be equally apt, but there the connexion is less certain. Like the Gigantomachy, the Greek victories over Amazons and Centaurs have been interpreted as symbols of the triumph of civilization, of man over brute, of the higher over the lower;[16] as for the Sack of Troy, in the fifth century some Greeks, at least, saw the Trojan War as an early episode in the struggle between Greece and the East, in whose latest phase Athens had played so great a part.[17] It might then be argued that the North, West, and South metopes have as their common element the exaltation of Greek ideals and Greek civilization, but this interpretation may go beyond the thought of the period, and in any case, as so much of the two long sides is missing or obscure, its foundations are insecure. As for the frieze, its subject, though singularly apposite, is remarkable, for in fifth-century Greece to represent the human world on a sacred building was an innovation, and a bold one. Various considerations may have prompted the choice. Religious festivals played an important part in the life of Athens, and there are indications that Pericles made some use of them as an instrument of domestic policy;[18] moreover, Athens required the cities under her control to send representatives and victims to take part in the Panathenaic procession,[19] for to the Greek mind a religious bond was a natural supplement to administrative and judicial ties. Thus the procession portrays not Athens alone but her whole empire, that empire whose funds helped to finance the Parthenon and were to be kept in it; it may even be that the temple was originally envisaged as an imperial shrine, in the belief that loyalty and spontaneous devotion, not coercion and the stress of war, would shape the future of the confederacy: but here we desert fact for speculation.

To sum up, it seems possible to detect in the frieze and pediments the characteristic manifestations of a single powerful and original mind; for the metopes the indications are less clear, and one must suppose that if the same man did in fact play a part in their creation, his influence was more restricted. The features of this unmistakable personality accord with what we know of Pheidias and his work, so although the positive evidence for the identification is not of the strongest, we must admit the plausibility of the long-established opinion which assigns to Pheidias the major share of the credit for the sculpture of the Parthenon.

NOTES

1. The programme was unsuccessfully resisted by Pericles' political opponents as a discreditable misuse of League funds (Plutarch, *Life of Pericles* XII).

    The statement of Isocrates (XV, 234), that Pericles so adorned Athens that later visitors felt she was worthy to rule not only the Greeks but the rest of mankind, is doubtless a rhetorical exaggeration; more soberly, Thucydides (I, 10) observes that whereas later generations would think Sparta's reputation inflated in the light of the remains of her public buildings, those of Athens would suggest that the city's power had been double the actuality.

2. In accordance with ancient practice the commission recorded its accounts on a slab of marble. Many pieces of this inscription have survived, and the slab itself has been reconstructed (A. M. Woodward, *Annual of the British School at Athens* XVI, 1909–10, 187 f; W. B. Dinsmoor, *American Journal of Archaeology* XVII, 1913, 53 f; XXV, 1921, 233 f). The date of the dedication of the Parthenos is given by an emended reading of the ancient commentary on Aristophanes, *Peace*, 605.

3. See *American Journal of Archaeology* LVIII, 1954, 144 f, for the summary of a paper by Professor Dinsmoor on certain indications that the West frieze may have been carved on the building.

4. See the summary referred to in the last note.

5. See the account by A. H. Smith in *Journal of Hellenic Studies* XXXVI, 1916, 163 f.

6. The interpretation is not beyond all doubt; A. H. Smith pointed out that none of the extant figures is clearly feminine (*The Sculptures of the Parthenon*, 44).

7. C. Praschniker, *Parthenonstudien* (Vienna, 1928), is a detailed study of the remains of the metopes on the North and East sides.

8. G. P. Stevens, 'The Setting of the Periclean Parthenon', *Hesperia*, Supplement III, 1940; 'The Periclean Entrance Court of the Acropolis of Athens', *Hesperia* V, 1936, 443 f. In *Hesperia* XV, 1946, 2 and 74, the same author gives a reconstructed drawing and a photograph of a model of the Acropolis in the first century B.C.

9. Pausanias I, 24, 5.

10. Figures 3–6 are based on drawings in the Bibliothèque Nationale which were made in 1674 by an artist in the suite of the Marquis de Nointel, French Ambassador to Turkey. See also R. Carpenter, 'New Material for the West Pediment of the Parthenon', *Hesperia* I, 1932, 1 f.; 'The Lost Statues of the East Pediment of the Parthenon', *Hesperia* II, 1933, 1 f; 'The Ostia Altar and the East Pediment of the Parthenon', *Hesperia*, Supplement VIII, 1949, 71 f.

11. Figure 7 is based on a drawing by R. Schneider, *Die Geburt der Athena* (*Abhandlungen des Arch.-Epig. Seminares der Universität Wien;* Vienna, 1880). See also *Hesperia* II, 1933, 1 f.

12. J. Overbeck, *Berichte der K. Sächs. Gesellschaft der Wissenschaften,* 1880, 42 f; 163 f. B. Sauer, *Athenische Mitteilungen* XVI, 1891, 59 f.

13. Plutarch, *Life of Pericles* XIII. Professor Dinsmoor has shown that in addition to the buildings enumerated by Plutarch, the Hephaesteum and the temple of Ares in Athens, the temple of Poseidon at Sunium, and the temple of Nemesis at Rhamnus were also constructed during this period (*Hesperia* IX, 1940, 47 f.).

14. G. M. A. Richter, *The Sculpture and Sculptors of the Greeks* (New Haven, 1950), 232.

15. The position will doubtless be much improved when the recent discoveries at Olympia are published; see *Journal of Hellenic Studies* 75, 1955, *Archaeology in Greece*, 12.

16. So T. B. L. Webster, *Greek Interpretations* (Manchester, 1942), 54 f; C. J. Herington, *Athena Parthenos and Athena Polias* (Manchester, 1955), 60 f.

17. Herodotus I, 1–5.

18. Plutarch, Life of *Pericles* XI, 4; for a specific addition made by Pericles to the Panathenaic festival, *ibid.* XIII, 9.

19. See the inscription discussed in *Hesperia* XIII, 1944, 1 f; also *Inscriptiones Graecae* I², 10, 2–4; 45, 11–12; 63, 57.

BIBLIOGRAPHY

A. Michaelis, *Der Parthenon* (Leipzig, 1871) is still fundamental, especially for the ancient literary and epigraphical evidence available at the time. For a general account of the temple and its architecture, see W. B. Dinsmoor, *The Architecture of Ancient Greece* (London and New York, 1950), which includes a bibliography for the Parthenon and the Acropolis in general; also D. S. Robertson, *A Handbook of Greek and Roman Architecture* (2nd ed., Cambridge, 1945). On the significance of the temple and the Parthenos, C. J. Herington, *Athena Parthenos and Athena Polias* (Manchester, 1955). Large-scale publication of the sculpture in A. H. Smith, *The Sculptures of the Parthenon* (London, 1910) and M. Collignon, *Le Parthenon* (Paris, 1912). For pictures of the temple and the greater part of the West frieze, W. Hege and G. Rodenwaldt, *The Acropolis* (Oxford, 1930). The style discussed by Ch. Picard, *Manuel d'Archéologie Grecque; La Sculpture* II (Paris, 1939) ch. 4; G. von Lücken, *Die Entwicklung der Parthenonskulpturen* (Augsburg, 1930); B. Schweitzer, *Jahrbuch des Deutschen Archäologischen Instituts* LIII, 1938, 1 f; LIV, 1939, 1 f; LV, 1940, 170 f; G. Becatti, *Problemi Fidiaci* (Milan–Florence, 1951); the last-named is especially useful for its illustrations of comparative material. For recent additions to the figures from the pediments see the articles by F. Brommer and E. B. Harrison in *Hesperia* XXIV, 1955, 85 f; by F. Brommer in *Festschrift zum 60. Geburtstag von Bernhard Schweitzer* (Stuttgart, 1954), 181 f; and in *Athenische Mitteilungen* 69/70, 1954/5, 49 f, and 71, 1956, 30 f; and by J. Marcadé in *Bulletin de Correspondance Hellénique* 80, 1956, 161 f. On the last, see Brommer, *Marburger Winckelmannprogramm* 1957, 7 f.

LIST OF PLATES

THE plates include only a part of the surviving material; four metopes, selected figures from the two pediments, and the better-preserved portions of the frieze. For a complete publication the reader is referred to the works of A. H. Smith and M. Collignon which are given in the bibliography. All the sculpture is in the British Museum except where otherwise stated; where the photographer's name is not given, the pictures are from Museum negatives. Where possible the pictures reproduced are from the originals, but fourteen slabs of the West frieze are illustrated from casts made by Lord Elgin's agents early in the last century, when some details were less weathered than they are today. The numbering of the metopes and the slabs of the frieze is taken from A. Michaelis and A. H. Smith.

steward on **slab** VI is from the same mould as the other figures on the slab; the original was destroyed with them.

14–15. A. North frieze. Slab II; part of slab IV; slabs V and VI; sacrificial heifers; a steward with a youth bearing a tray of offerings; youths with water-jars. Slabs II and VI are in the Acropolis Museum (*Alinari* 24638 and 24628).

B. North frieze. Slabs X, XI, and XII; old men; stewards and a chariot. Slab X is a cast; the original is in the Acropolis Museum. Slab XI is in the Acropolis Museum (*Alinari* 24634).

16–17. A. North frieze. Slabs XVII, XVIII, XXII, and XXIII; chariots and stewards. Slab XVII is in the Acropolis Museum (*Alinari* 24629). The lower part of slab XXII is a cast; the original is in the Acropolis Museum.

B. North frieze. Slabs XXIX, XXXI, XXXII, and part of XXXIII; parade of cavalry. Slab XXXI is in the Acropolis Museum (*Alinari* 24633).

18–19. A. North frieze. Slabs XXXIII, XXXIV, XXXV, and XXXVI; parade of cavalry.

B. North frieze. Slabs XXXVII, XXXVIII, XXXIX, and part of XL; parade of cavalry.

20–21. A. North frieze. Part of slab XL; slabs XLI and XLII; parade of cavalry. West frieze. Slab I; a steward.

B. West frieze. Slabs II, III, and IV; cavalrymen preparing for parade. Slabs III and IV are casts; the originals are on the Parthenon.

22–23. A. West frieze. Slabs V, VI, and VII; cavalrymen preparing for parade. From casts; the originals are on the Parthenon.

B. West frieze. Slabs VIII, IX, and X; cavalrymen preparing for parade. From casts; the originals are on the Parthenon.

24–25. A. West frieze. Slabs XI, XII, and XIII; cavalrymen preparing for parade. From casts; the originals are on the Parthenon.

B. West frieze. Slabs XIV, XV, and XVI; cavalrymen preparing for parade. From casts; the originals are on the Parthenon.

26. South frieze. Slab XXV; a chariot, an armed man, and a steward.

27. South frieze. Detail from slab XL; head of a heifer (*Baer*).

28. East frieze. Part of slab VI; Poseidon, Apollo and Artemis (*Alinari* 24631).

29. North frieze. Slab XXXVIII; cavalry.

30. East frieze. Part of slab VII; a steward with two girls (*Sougez*).

31. West frieze. Detail from slab II; mounted youth (*Baer*).

32. West frieze. Slab VIII; a man controlling a restive horse. From a cast; the original is on the Parthenon.

33. West pediment. Reclining river god.

34. West pediment. Part of the head and torso of Athena. The neck and head are casts; the originals are in Athens.

A

X   XI

B

XXV   XXX

6

A

B

XII XIII

XLI

7

A

XXXIX　　　　　　　　　　XL

B

I　　　　　　II　　　　　　　　III

8

XXXVIII

A

III   IV

B

V

10

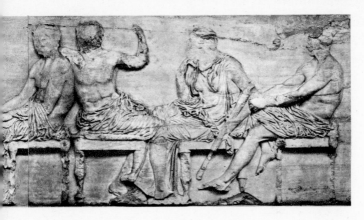

A

B

11

A

VI

B

VI   VII

A

B

VIII

13

A

II   IV

B

X   XI

14

VI

XII

A

XVII   XVIII

B

XXIX   XXXI

16

XXII   XXIII

XXXII   XXXIII

A

XXXIII   XXXIV   XXXV

B

XXXVII   XXXVIII

18

A

XXXVI

B

XXXIX   XL

19

A

XL   XLI

B

II   I

20

A

I   I

B

IV

21

A

V   VI

B

VIII   IX

22

A

VII

B

X

A

XI   XII

B

XIV   XV

24

A

XIII

B

XVI

25

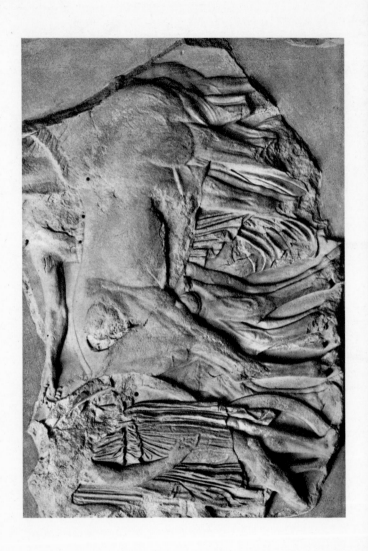

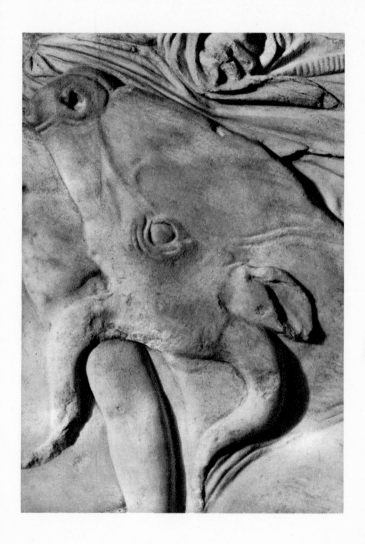

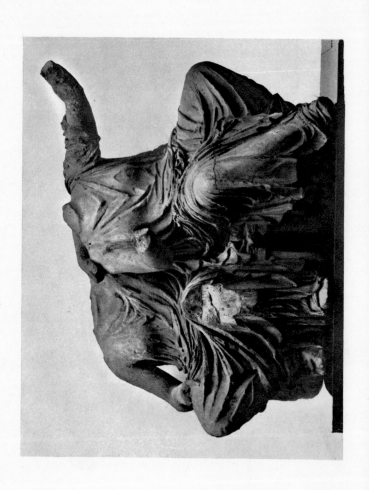